D0801575

LEVEL
3

September 11

Libby Romero

NATIONAL
GEOGRAPHIC

Washington, D.C.

For my family —L.R.

Published by National Geographic Partners, LLC, Washington, DC 20036.

Designed by Anne LeongSon

Trade paperback ISBN: 978-1-4263-7218-6
Reinforced library binding ISBN:
978-1-4263-7219-3

Author's Note

The author and publisher gratefully acknowledge the expert content review of this book by Ian Kerrigan, senior vice president for exhibitions, and Katherine Fleming, exhibition research specialist, both of the 9/11 Memorial & Museum; the review of Bridget Petrites, library assistant, Evanston Public Library, Evanston, IL; the fact-checking review by Michelle Harris; as well as the literacy review by Mariam Jean Dreher, professor emerita of reading education, University of Maryland, College Park.

Note From the 9/11 Memorial & Museum

There are so many lessons tied to September 11 —it is difficult to understand the world we live in today without understanding what happened on 9/11. On that day and for months afterward, ordinary people responded in extraordinary ways with acts of selflessness and empathy in the face of unimaginable violence. In doing so, they serve as inspiration today for children as well as adults when we again find ourselves in challenging times.

Photo Credits

GI: Getty Images; SS: Shutterstock
Cover, Jim Young/Reuters; 1, U.S. Navy Photo by Jim Watson; 3, Daniel Thornberg/Adobe Stock; 4–5, Jeremy Woodhouse/GI; 6–7, David Surowiecki/GI; 7, vanbeets/GI; 8, Carmen Taylor/AP Photo; 9, Spencer Platt/GI; 10–11, Navy Photo by Petty Officer 1st Class Mark D. Faram; 11, AP Photo/SS; 12, NG Maps, data from the Federal Bureau of Investigation; 12–13, David Maxwell/AFP via GI; 14, Spencer Platt/GI; 15, Stuart Clarke/SS; 16–17, Jose Jimenez/Primera Hora/GI; 18, Henny Ray Abrams/AFP via GI; 19 (UP), Paul Hawthorne/AP/SS; 19 (LO), Claus Lunau/Science Source; 20 (UP), Pat Carroll/NY Daily News Archive via GI; 20 (LO), Tamara Beckwith/The New York Post; 21, Lm Otero/AP/SS; 22 (UP), U.S. Navy Photo by Preston Keres; 22 (LO), Bernard Weil/Toronto Star via GI; 23, 2001 The Record (Bergen Co., NJ)/GI; 24, Andrew Lichtenstein/Corbis via GI; 25, Everett/SS; 26–27, Det. Greg Semendinger, NYC Police Aviation Unit/NYPD/New York City Police Foundation; 28, U.S. Navy Photo by Preston Keres; 29 (UP), Andrea Booher/SS; 29 (LO), Stephen Chernin/AP Photo; 30 (UP), Bettmann/GI; 30 (CTR), Porter Gifford/Corbis via GI; 30 (LO), Everett/SS; 31 (UP), Damian Dovarganes/AP/SS; 31 (CTR), Digital Vision/GI; 31 (LO LE), IndustryAndTravel/SS; 31 (LO RT), Andrea Booher/FEMA News Photo; 32–33, Doug Mills/AP/SS; 34, Richard Corkery/NY Daily News Archive via GI; 35, Robert Lachman/Los Angeles Times via GI; 36, Anthony Harvey/GI; 37, Roslan Rahman/AFP via GI; 38, courtesy of NAV CANADA; 39, Scott Cook/The Canadian Press; 40, Steve Heap/SS; 41 (UP), Justin Lane-Pool/GI; 41 (LO), James Kirkikis/SS; 42–43, Sean Pavone/SS; 43, Drew Angerer/GI; 44 (LE), Andre Nantel/SS; 44 (RT), Ivan Cholakov/GI; 45 (UP), courtesy of NYC Office Of Emergency Management/GI; 45 (CTR UP LE), Gregory Reed/SS; 45 (CTR UP RT), Cliff Schiappa/AP/SS; 45 (CTR LO LE), Joseph Sohm/SS; 45 (CTR LO RT), Universal History Archive/UIG/SS; 45 (LO), Steve Heap/SS; 46 (UP LE), Daniel Thornberg/Adobe Stock; 46 (UP RT), Robert Giroux/GI; 46 (CTR LE), Richard Corkery/NY Daily News Archive via GI; 46 (CTR RT), Anthony Harvey/GI; 46 (LO LE), shinji miyamoto/SS; 46 (LO RT), Steve Heap/SS; 47 (UP LE), Yanukit/Adobe Stock; 47 (UP RT), Spencer Platt/GI; 47 (CTR LE), 2001 The Record (Bergen Co., NJ)/GI; 47 (CTR RT), courtesy of NYC Office Of Emergency Management/GI; 47 (LO LE), Digital Vision/GI; 47 (LO RT), vanbeets/GI

National Geographic supports K–12 educators with ELA Common Core Resources. Visit natgeoed.org/commoncore for more information.

Contents

Tuesday Morning

On September 11, 2001, people on the East Coast of the United States woke up to a beautiful late summer day. The sun shone brightly in a brilliant blue sky. It was a Tuesday, and people in New York City were preparing for another day at work and school.

The twin towers soar over New York City before September 11, 2001.

Thousands of people headed for the twin towers that morning. These two skyscrapers were part of the World Trade Center. They rose above the city's downtown skyline on the island of Manhattan. Nobody knew the world was about to change.

twin towers

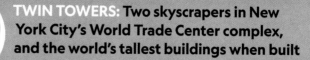

Word to KNOW

TWIN TOWERS: Two skyscrapers in New York City's World Trade Center complex, and the world's tallest buildings when built

A Shocking Event

New York is a loud, busy city with three major airports nearby. People who live there are used to seeing and hearing airplanes flying overhead. But on this morning, people stopped on the street and looked up. The sound of the airplane was too loud. The airplane they saw was flying too low. And to their horror, the airplane flew straight into the side of the north tower of the World Trade Center.

American Airlines Flight 11 hit the north tower at 8:46 a.m. The impact of the crash tore a hole that stretched from the 93rd to 99th floors of the building.

World Trade Center

The World Trade Center contained seven buildings. The twin towers, also known as the north and south towers, were the tallest. Each had 110 stories and stood about 1,360 feet high. In 2001, between 30,000 and 50,000 people worked at the World Trade Center every weekday. Tens of thousands more passed through the complex. Subway cars and other trains went under and near the World Trade Center. Experts estimate that more than 130,000 people traveled on them each day.

HEROES in ACTION

Flight attendants Betty Ann Ong and Madeline Amy Sweeney called American Airlines from aboard Flight 11 before the plane crashed. They reported that the plane was in trouble.

Smoke and flames poured out of the building. Many people thought they had just seen a terrible accident. But 17 minutes later, a second plane flew into one of the World Trade Center buildings— this time into the south tower.

Many cameras caught the second attack on film. The video was played over and over again on television. Soon people knew that hijackers had taken over the planes. A group of men had taken control of the cockpit of each airplane and flown them into the buildings on purpose.

People were watching the fire in the north tower when a second plane flew toward the south tower.

Word to KNOW

HIJACKER: A person who takes over an aircraft, ship, or vehicle with force or the threat of force

United Airlines Flight 175 crashed into the 77th through 85th floors of the south tower at 9:03 a.m.

The Attack Continues

The United States was under attack, and the attack was not yet over. About half an hour later, hijackers crashed a third airplane. This plane hit the west side of the Pentagon in Arlington, Virginia. As it sliced through the concrete building, the plane instantly broke into tiny pieces. The plane's fuel tanks exploded and two giant fireballs blasted into the air.

Hijackers crashed American Airlines Flight 77 into the Pentagon, causing explosions and fires.

Who Was Behind the Attacks?

The hijackers who committed the 9/11 attacks were part of a terrorist, or violent rebel, group. In 2001, this group, called al Qaeda (alk-EYE-duh), was based in Afghanistan (af-GAN-ih-stan). Their leader was Osama bin Laden (oh-SAH-mah BIN LAH-dun). Al Qaeda considered the United States to be its enemy. The hijackers used the airplanes to attack important American buildings. Over many years, al Qaeda trained members and planned violent attacks on people, buildings, and ships in countries around the world.

In total, 19 hijackers took over the planes that crashed on 9/11.

The U.S. government ordered all airplanes flying over the country to land as soon as possible. But it was too late for United Airlines Flight 93. Hijackers had already taken control of this fourth aircraft. They were flying the plane toward Washington, D.C.

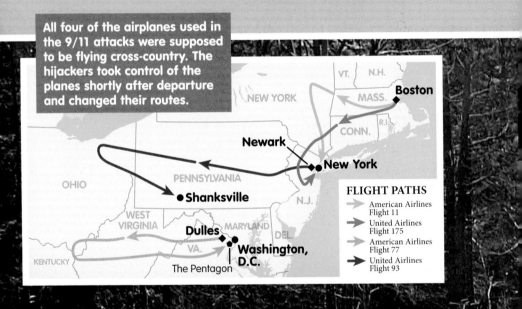

All four of the airplanes used in the 9/11 attacks were supposed to be flying cross-country. The hijackers took control of the planes shortly after departure and changed their routes.

FLIGHT PATHS

American Airlines Flight 11

United Airlines Flight 175

American Airlines Flight 77

United Airlines Flight 93

Passengers and crew members called loved ones, who told them about the other attacks. People on Flight 93 thought their aircraft would be used as a weapon, too. So they fought the hijackers to try to get control of the plane. In response, the hijackers crashed the plane into a field in Pennsylvania.

HERO in ACTION

In a phone call recorded as passengers and crew began to fight back, passenger Todd Beamer was heard saying, "Are you ready? Okay, let's roll."

Flight 93 crashed into a field near Shanksville, Pennsylvania. The crash site is a short flight away from the hijackers' likely target, a building in Washington, D.C.

The Rescue Begins

Many people escaped from the twin towers. But others were trapped inside the burning buildings.

In New York City , dark smoke poured from the twin towers. People rushed to escape the area, which later became known as ground zero.

In some cases, brave co-workers saved people's lives. Rick Rescorla was vice president of security at a company with offices on floors 43 to 74 of the south tower. After the first plane struck the north tower, Rescorla immediately ordered

HERO in ACTION
Rick Rescorla made his co-workers regularly practice escape drills. Knowing what to do saved their lives on 9/11.

everyone in his office to leave. He used a bullhorn so people could hear him. He helped nearly 2,700 people make it down the stairs to safety.

Word to KNOW

GROUND ZERO: A term once used to identify the site where the 9/11 World Trade Center attacks and recovery in New York City took place

First responders—including police officers, firefighters, and paramedics—arrived within minutes of the first attack on the World Trade Center in New York City. They rushed in to help. They knew they had a massive rescue operation before them.

Almost all of the elevators in the twin towers had stopped working. In the higher floors, many stairs were blocked by rubble or fire. People who were able to escape headed down the stairs that were still open. On the way down, they passed firefighters who were climbing up to search for survivors.

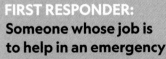

Word to KNOW

FIRST RESPONDER:
Someone whose job is to help in an emergency

HERO in ACTION

In the north tower, Port Authority Police Department captain Kathy Mazza was said to have broken glass walls near an exit. This helped hundreds of people escape.

On September 11, thousands of first responders risked their lives to save others. Here, firefighters rush to the scene.

The Towers Fall

Many of those firefighters didn't make it out. When the airplanes hit the twin towers, they caused massive damage. Concrete floors were destroyed. Steel support beams were cut in two.

The twin towers fell on the morning of 9/11. After burning for hours, a third building—7 World Trade Center—collapsed later that day.

Floors above the crash sites started to sag downward. Meanwhile, the sprinklers in both buildings were damaged. There was nothing to stop the raging fires, which became hot enough to weaken steel.

The collapse of the twin towers caused huge dust clouds. Here, people run from the area, trying to escape.

The buildings grew unstable. Then they collapsed.

Why Did the Towers Collapse?

The twin towers had already survived one attack. In 1993, terrorists exploded a bomb in a parking garage beneath the World Trade Center. The bomb was close to the north tower and caused damage to the building. So why did the towers collapse on 9/11? The planes that hit them were full of fuel. All that fuel caused fires that burned so hot that the steel holding up the buildings weakened. The buildings' floors crashed down upon each other, all the way to the ground.

1. 9:59 a.m. south tower falls
2. 10:28 a.m. north tower falls
3. 5:20 p.m. 7 World Trade Center falls

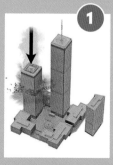

Once the south tower began to crumble, it took only 10 seconds for it to collapse.

The south tower fell first. Six firefighters from New York City Fire Department Ladder Company 6 were in the north tower when it happened. The impact caused the north tower to shake. The firefighters needed to leave before the north tower fell, too.

HEROES in ACTION
The firefighters of Ladder Company 6 called Josephine Harris their "guardian angel." They knew that if they had been anywhere else in the building or just outside it, the building would have fallen on top of them.

When the north tower fell, it "peeled away like a banana" around a tiny section of stairs.

As they rushed down the stairs, they found Josephine Harris. She had climbed down at least 50 flights of stairs and could not go on. The firefighters helped her. When they got near the bottom, the north tower crumbled. Only the small bit of twisted stairwell around them was left standing, protecting them from being crushed.

First responders helped many people escape before the twin towers collapsed. More than 25,000 people made it out of the buildings. Sadly, between the twin towers, the Pentagon, and the people on the four airplanes, nearly 3,000 people died during the 9/11 attacks.

Four days after the 9/11 attacks, a New York City firefighter signals that 10 more rescue workers are needed in the rubble at ground zero.

The Little Church That Stood

St. Paul's Chapel, built in 1766, is Manhattan's oldest church. It sits right across the street from the World Trade Center. Amazingly, it was not damaged when the giant towers fell. None of its windows were even broken! For nearly nine months after the attacks, the church gave meals, a place to sleep, and comfort to people working at ground zero. Visitors posted flags, letters, and other mementos on the chapel's fence. Today, St. Paul's remains a symbol of hope and recovery.

St. Paul's Chapel

Firefighters raise a flag in front of rubble at ground zero.

The Rescue Continues

After the towers fell, clouds of debris rained down on the city. People near the attack site were covered with dust and powdery gray ash. Thousands of people flooded the streets, running away from downtown.

People escape by walking across the Manhattan Bridge.

Many people wanted to get out of Manhattan. Some walked miles to reach bridges so they could leave. But after the planes hit, New York City was quickly shut down. Many bridges, roads, and tunnels were closed to traffic in case there was another attack. The subway system shut down. Many train lines stopped running. Some buses were rerouted to pick up people fleeing Lower Manhattan.

Lower Manhattan was filled with dust after the twin towers fell.

Large crowds headed away from the World Trade Center. To the south, people fled to a park on the tip of Manhattan. The Coast Guard sent out a call for help. It asked all boats in the area to take people to safety. More than 150 ferries, yachts (YOTTS), tour boats, and tugboats responded.

Despite the fear of another attack, many boat captains rushed to Lower Manhattan to rescue people.

In less than nine hours, the boats rescued up to 500,000 people. They took people to Staten Island, Ellis Island, and across the river to New Jersey. It was the largest water rescue operation in American history.

Dogs in Action

In the days after the attacks, thousands of rescuers searched for people in the rubble of the World Trade Center. More than 300 dogs joined them.

Dogs like Riley were an important part of the rescue operation. They could search faster than humans. They could also go places people couldn't go.

A black Labrador retriever named Billy searches for victims at ground zero.

Trakr and his handler were one of the first search and rescue teams to arrive at the World Trade Center site.

Working with their human handlers, many of the specially trained dogs sniffed and searched. The heroic canines worked up to 12 hours a day. One dog, a German shepherd named Trakr, found Genelle Guzman-McMillan. She had been pinned under a pile of steel and cement for 27 hours. She was the last survivor rescued from ground zero.

In addition to searching, service dogs also comforted first responders as they completed their hard and dangerous job.

7 IMPORTANT FACTS

1 It took **three years** (from 1968 to 1971) to **build** the steel framework of the twin towers. It took only **102 minutes** for both towers to **collapse** in 2001.

2 It took workers nearly **nine months** to complete recovery, cleanup, and evidence gathering at **ground zero.**

3 Astronaut Frank Culbertson was on the **International Space Station** on 9/11. Photos he took from space show **smoke rising above Manhattan.**

4

After the north tower was hit, a guide dog named Roselle led her blind owner and several other people down 78 stories to safety.

5

The section of the Pentagon that was hit on 9/11 had just been updated. Many lives were saved because people hadn't moved back into those offices yet.

6

A new skyscraper, One World Trade Center, opened on the World Trade Center site in 2014. At 1,776 feet, it's the tallest building in the Western Hemisphere.

7

Many people in the U.S. hadn't heard of disaster search dogs or therapy dogs before 9/11. The dogs' usefulness during this disaster changed that.

The Official Response

President George W. Bush visits ground zero in New York on September 14, 2001.

The events of September 11, 2001, shook the nation. And the government had to respond. President George W. Bush led the country in a day of prayer and remembrance. Then he led the nation's effort to find and punish the people who had caused the attacks and to prevent new ones. World leaders came together. They promised to help the United States.

"Terrorist attacks can shake the foundations of our biggest buildings, but they cannot touch the foundation of America. These acts shattered steel, but they cannot dent the steel of American resolve."

—President George W. Bush's address to the nation
September 11, 2001

In October 2001, the U.S. and its allies (AL-eyes) started military actions in Afghanistan. They were searching for members of al Qaeda who were responsible for the 9/11 attacks. Nearly 10 years later in May 2011, they finally found the group's leader, Osama bin Laden, in nearby Pakistan.

Word to KNOW

ALLY: A person, group, or nation that works with another for a specific purpose

Banding Together

After the attacks, many people in the U.S. wanted to show support for their country. American flags flew everywhere. Many people gave flowers, candles, food, and notes of thanks to first responders.

Rock legend Paul McCartney organized the Concert for New York City. It lasted for five hours and helped raise $35 million for victims of the 9/11 attacks.

People and groups also gave money, donating a record-breaking $2.8 billion to help victims of the attacks. By the end of 2001, more than 300 charities were raising money for the cause.

Words to KNOW

DONATE: To give time, money, or goods

CHARITY: A group that gives help or raises money for those in need

Americans came together to show their patriotism and support after 9/11.

Anger and Fear

Most Americans tried to help others after the 9/11 attacks. But some people took their anger and fear out on people who looked like they came from the same countries as the hijackers. Innocent people, who had nothing to do with the events of 9/11, were sometimes attacked and not treated fairly.

People gather by a pile of flowers outside the U.S. Embassy in London after the 9/11 attacks.

The 9/11 attacks took place in America, but they affected people all around the world. In many countries, people brought flowers to U.S. embassies. They lit candles to honor the victims. They gathered to sing "The Star-Spangled Banner," the U.S. national anthem. They donated money and supplies, and offered support.

Word to KNOW

EMBASSY: The official residence or office of an ambassador who represents their government in a foreign country

People light candles at the U.S. Embassy in Singapore to honor those who were lost.

One French newspaper showed its support with the front-page headline "*Nous sommes tous Américains.*" That means, "We are all Americans." Many people felt that an attack on the United States was an attack on all countries.

At 11 a.m. on September 13, 2001, millions of people around Europe stopped what they were doing. They were silent for three minutes to honor victims of the 9/11 attacks.

One place that pitched in to help was Gander, Newfoundland, in Canada. On 9/11, airplanes were told to land as soon as possible. No planes could fly over or into the United States. For 38 large airliners, the closest landing spot was the little airport in this small Canadian town.

Planes park along the runway at the Gander airport, near the northeastern tip of Newfoundland.

Stranded passengers are made comfortable and given a place to sleep in a Gander school.

For the next five days, residents of Gander and nearby towns took care of almost 7,000 passengers and crew members from about 100 countries. When hotel rooms filled up, people let passengers move into their homes. They gave them food, clothing, and phones to call their loved ones. They asked for nothing in return.

Gander International Airport wasn't built to handle so many large aircraft at one time. As the heavy planes sat, they slowly sank into the runway.

20 Years Later

Much has changed since September 11, 2001. For one thing, air travel is much safer. All passengers and bags are now checked to make sure people do not bring anything harmful on an airplane.

At the attack sites, the rubble has been cleared. Memorials now honor those who lost their lives. But for anyone old enough to recall that day, 9/11 is an event that is impossible to forget.

Word to KNOW

MEMORIAL: Something built or created to remind others of a person or event

The Tower of Voices at the Flight 93 National Memorial in Pennsylvania has 40 wind chimes to honor the plane's passengers and crew members.

The 9/11 Memorial & Museum in New York City contains pools set within each area where the twin towers stood.

Each of the 184 benches at the National 9/11 Pentagon Memorial is dedicated to a victim of the attack.

The attacks on September 11, 2001, shook America. They made people realize that even a powerful country like the U.S. could be a victim of violence. But the attacks also brought Americans closer together. As U.S. senator John Kerry said at the time, "It was the worst day we have ever seen, but it brought out the best in all of us."

Every year on September 11, twin towers of light shine up to the sky in New York City.

QUIZ WHIZ

How much do you know about September 11, 2001? After reading this book, probably a lot. Take this quiz and find out.

Answers are at the bottom of page 45.

1 How many planes were hijacked on September 11, 2001?
A. one
B. two
C. three
D. four

2 In which city did the first attacks take place?
A. Washington, D.C.
B. New York City
C. Arlington, Virginia
D. Shanksville, Pennsylvania

3 Which building was hit first?
A. the north tower of the World Trade Center
B. the south tower of the World Trade Center
C. the Pentagon
D. the U.S. Capitol

4 What did people call the attack and recovery site where the twin towers once stood?

A. Area 51
B. Ladder 6
C. ground zero
D. first responder

5 _____ was president of the United States on September 11, 2001.

A. Barack Obama
B. George W. Bush
C. Bill Clinton
D. Ronald Reagan

6 A _____ found the last survivor rescued in New York.

A. firefighter
B. police officer
C. paramedic
D. dog

7 Which 9/11 memorial has wind chimes?

A. the 9/11 Memorial & Museum in New York
B. the National 9/11 Pentagon Memorial
C. the Flight 93 National Memorial
D. the World Trade Center

GLOSSARY

9/11: Another name for the terrorist attacks that took place on September 11, 2001

DONATE: To give time, money, or goods

EMBASSY: The official residence or office of an ambassador who represents their government in a foreign country

HIJACKER: A person who takes over an aircraft, ship, or vehicle with force or the threat of force

MEMORIAL: Something built or created to remind others of a person or event

ALLY: A person, group, or nation that works with another for a specific purpose

CHARITY: A group that gives help or raises money for those in need

FIRST RESPONDER: Someone whose job is to help in an emergency

GROUND ZERO: A term once used to identify the site where the 9/11 World Trade Center attacks and recovery in New York City took place

PENTAGON: The five-sided building that serves as headquarters for the U.S. Department of Defense

TWIN TOWERS: Two skyscrapers in New York City's World Trade Center complex, and the world's tallest buildings when built

INDEX